What's inside?

World of snakes

Snakes have wriggly bodies covered with thousands of tiny scales. Snakes come in all sorts of colours and sizes. They live almost everywhere, from rocky mountains to sandy deserts. Some snakes slither along the ground, others dangle from trees.

whip snake

horned viper

Guess what?
Snakes like warm, sunny places. You'll never see a snake in the snow.

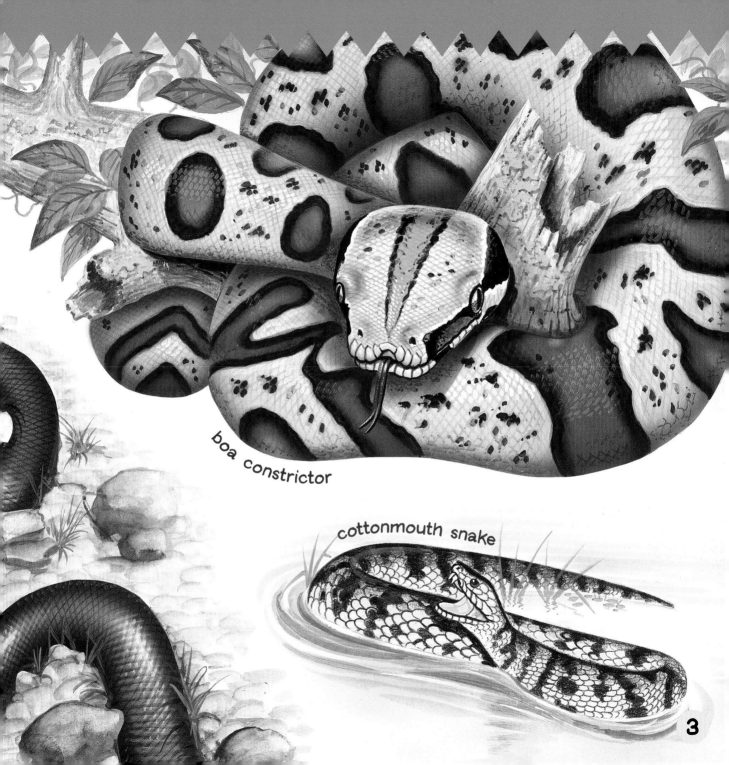

boa constrictor

cottonmouth snake

3

Python

A python is a huge, fat snake that can be as long as a bus. During the day, this large, green tree python coils itself up and snoozes in a leafy tree. At night, it slithers off and hunts for animals to fill its enormous belly.

ha ha

Why can't you play a joke on a snake? Because you can never pull its leg!

How heavy?

A python is much heavier than you are. It can weigh as much as seven children.

A python squeezes animals to death. It coils its super-strong body around a tasty animal and pulls tight.

A python opens its jaws so wide that it can gulp down a whole pig in one mouthful.

Once, a python was discovered with prickles sticking out of its tummy. The hungry snake had swallowed a spiky porcupine!

5

Lunch is ready

Snakes snack on all kinds of animals. Some eat their catch while it is still alive. Others kill their prey first by biting it with pointed teeth, called fangs. Most snakes open their jaws wide, then swallow the animal whole.

Guess what?
A snake may take up to half an hour to gulp down a whole animal.

Spitting snake
A black spitting cobra squirts deadly poison from its fangs. It can hit an animal up to three metres away.

Fiendish fangs

A viper creeps up on an animal and strikes with its sharp fangs. Powerful poison shoots through the fangs and into the victim's body.

Gone fishing

Water snakes feast on fish in their underwater home. Fish have lots of slippery scales that make them easy to swallow.

Egg head

An egg-eating snake swallows an egg whole. The hungry snake crushes the egg inside its body and sucks out the creamy yolk. Then it spits out the crunchy shell.

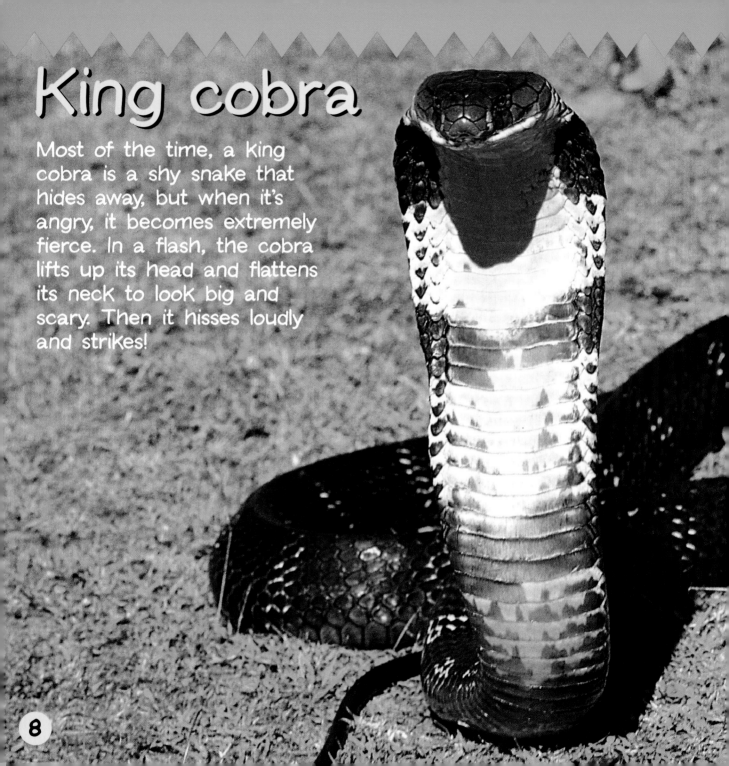

King cobra

Most of the time, a king cobra is a shy snake that hides away, but when it's angry, it becomes extremely fierce. In a flash, the cobra lifts up its head and flattens its neck to look big and scary. Then it hisses loudly and strikes!

ha ha
What's a snake's favourite subject?
Hiss-tory!

How long?

A king cobra is so long that four children could slide along its back at the same time.

Just like other snakes, a cobra smells food by flicking out its long tongue.

Some cobras can dance! When a snake charmer plays a flute, the cobra gently sways to and fro.

Even big elephants are scared of king cobras because these snakes are so poisonous.

9

Leave me alone

A hungry bird is always on the lookout for a snake to munch for its dinner. But snakes trick birds in many ways. They hide, play dead and even tie themselves in knots.

Copycat

A gentle milk snake is safe from predators because it looks like a deadly coral snake. Birds see its copycat markings and fly off.

Spot the snake

Can you see a snake hiding in this picture? The copperhead's blotchy markings make it look like dead leaves on the forest floor.

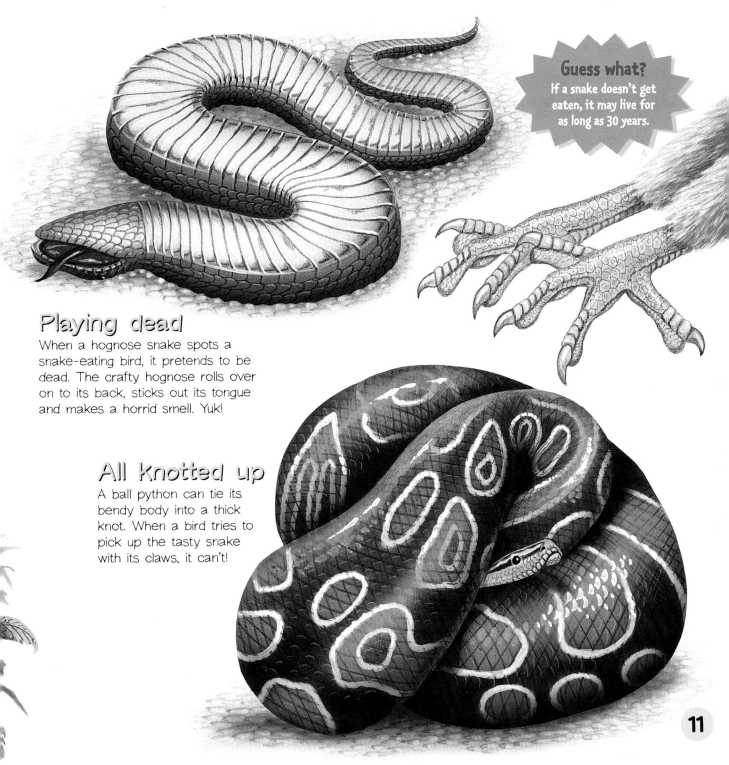

Playing dead

When a hognose snake spots a snake-eating bird, it pretends to be dead. The crafty hognose rolls over on to its back, sticks out its tongue and makes a horrid smell. Yuk!

All knotted up

A ball python can tie its bendy body into a thick knot. When a bird tries to pick up the tasty snake with its claws, it can't!

11

Rattlesnake

This large, noisy snake has a rattle at the tip of its tail. When it twitches its body, knobbly rings knock together and make a strange buzzing sound. Rattlesnakes live in dry, rocky places and are deadly poisonous.

ha ha
How does a snake sign its name?
Love and hisses!

How loud?

When a rattlesnake shakes its tail, it makes a noise as loud as a baby's rattle. If you can hear it, you're too close!

Rattlesnake facts

Animals are attracted by a rattlesnake's noisy tail. They don't notice that the snake is about to gobble them up!

A rattlesnake rests during the winter. When cold weather comes, it slinks into a rocky cave and dozes until spring.

Rattlesnakes wrestle each other to prove who's stronger. To win, a snake has to pin its enemy to the ground.

13

On the move

Have you ever seen a snake move? It grips the ground with its scaly belly and wriggles along. Some snakes climb trees, while others even seem to fly through the air.

Leaping snake

A paradise snake leaps from tree to tree like an acrobat. As it swings through the air, it wriggles and steers with its pointy tail.

Record breaker

A black mamba is the fastest snake. It races along at 19 kilometres per hour, which is faster than you can run. But it can't keep up the pace for long.

Twist and bend

A sidewinder moves across desert sand by flicking its body from side to side. Does the shape it makes remind you of a letter of the alphabet?

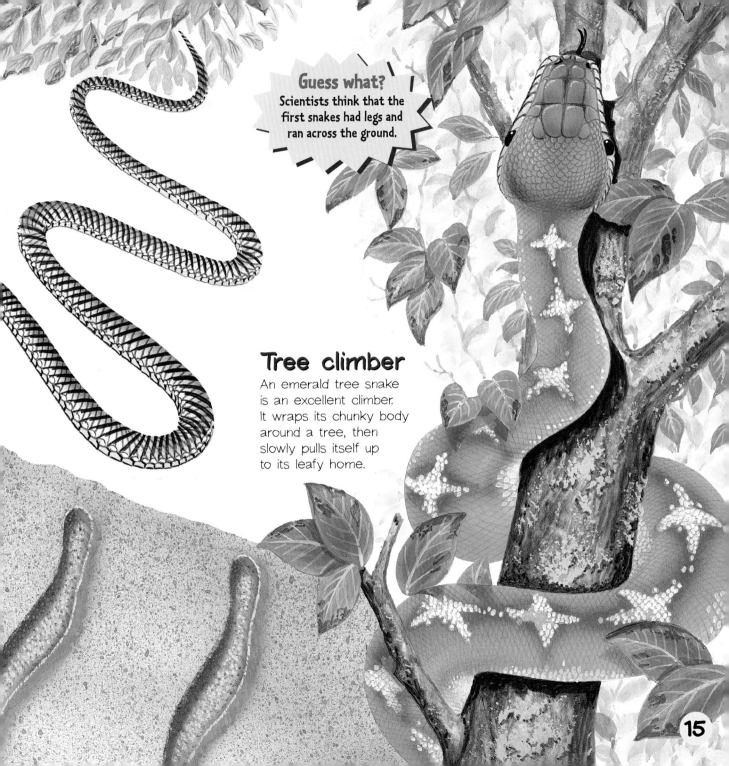

Tree climber

An emerald tree snake
is an excellent climber.
It wraps its chunky body
around a tree, then
slowly pulls itself up
to its leafy home.

Eggs and babies

A few snakes grow inside their mothers, but most hatch from eggs. A mother snake leaves her eggs under a bush, or inside a hollow tree, until the baby snakes are ready to pop out.

Break out

These baby green mambas are starting to hatch. They tear open their soft, leathery shells with a special tooth and slip out of the eggs.

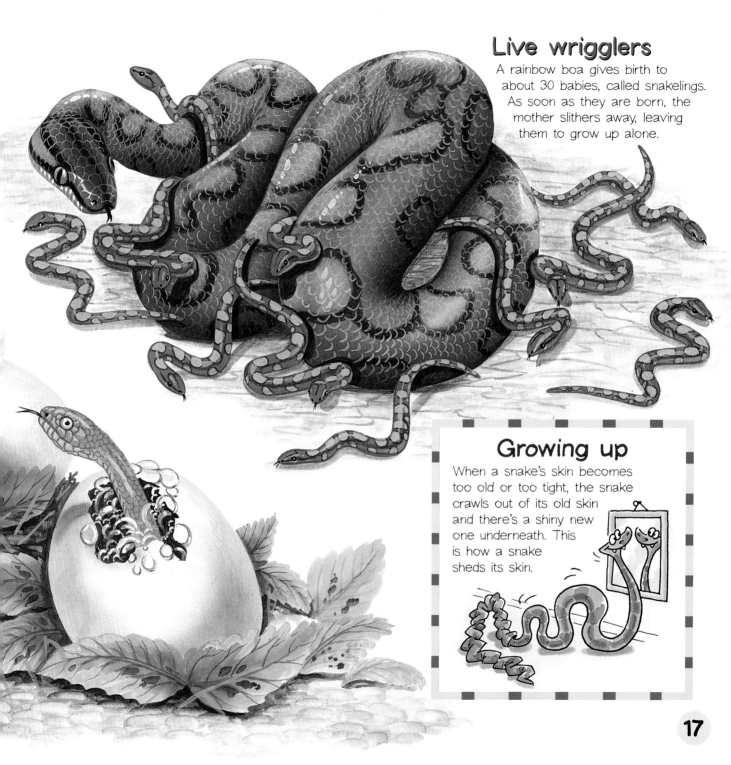

Live wrigglers

A rainbow boa gives birth to about 30 babies, called snakelings. As soon as they are born, the mother slithers away, leaving them to grow up alone.

Growing up

When a snake's skin becomes too old or too tight, the snake crawls out of its old skin and there's a shiny new one underneath. This is how a snake sheds its skin.

Can Snakes Hurt People?

Poisonous snakes can give you a nasty bite. Luckily it's easy to keep away from their fangs. Here's some useful advice...

1

If snakes live nearby, wear shoes, thick socks and long trousers to protect your legs. It's easy to step on a snake by mistake.

How do I stay safe?

HISSSSS

2

Don't poke under rocks or logs. Snakes may be hiding here and they like to be left alone.

A bit like my older sister!

DO NOT DISTURB

3

If a poisonous snake bites me, what should I do?

You need a special medicine, called antivenom. It's made with poison squeezed from a snake's fangs.

4

Hospitals keep many antivenoms. Each one matches a different type of snake. People also carry antivenom when they go hiking.

5

As soon as the doctor injects the antivenom into your arm, you start to feel better.

Phew!

A STRANGE PET

Of course, many snakes don't have poisonous fangs. These snakes are so gentle that people even keep them as pets.

Hi!

Fast facts

Here you can find out amazing facts about some of the snakes you have met already.

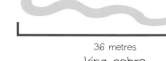

36 metres
king cobra

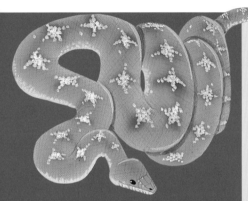

Tree python

Home: hanging from trees in steamy, hot rainforests.
Food: birds and bats
Colour: green, often with a pattern.
Is it poisonous? No
Special body parts: big front teeth for biting birds and a powerful body for squeezing its catch.
Amazing fact: a baby tree python is yellow or red until it's about eight months old.

King cobra

Home: among leaves or grasses in hot countries.
Food: snakes, birds and mice
Colour: brown, greenish-brown or black on top, cream or yellow underneath.
Is it poisonous? Yes
Special body parts: its neck spreads out into a hood when it feels threatened.
Amazing fact: a king cobra is an excellent climber. It can chase other snakes up trees.

Rattlesnake

Home: dry hillsides or woodlands
Food: birds, rats, mice and frogs
Colour: many different colours, often with a diamond pattern.
Is it poisonous? Yes
Special body parts: rings of dried skin at the end of its tail which make a noise like a rattle.
Amazing fact: a rattlesnake's fangs break easily. When a fang snaps, the snake grows a new one.

3 metres
black mamba

2 metres
rattlesnake

1.8 metres
tree python

1.5 metres
cottonmouth
snake

1.2 metres
child

0.6 metres
horned
viper

Cottonmouth snake

Home: in rivers and lakes
Food: frogs, fish, newts and tadpoles
Colour: yellow and black
Is it poisonous? Yes
Special body parts: the inside of its mouth is white, the colour of cotton wool.
Amazing fact: a cottonmouth snake warns that it's about to bite by opening its mouth wide.

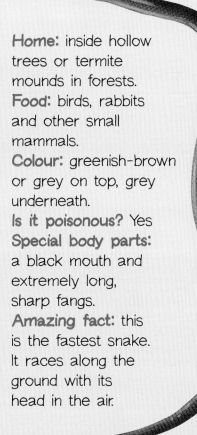

Black mamba

Home: inside hollow trees or termite mounds in forests.
Food: birds, rabbits and other small mammals.
Colour: greenish-brown or grey on top, grey underneath.
Is it poisonous? Yes
Special body parts: a black mouth and extremely long, sharp fangs.
Amazing fact: this is the fastest snake. It races along the ground with its head in the air.

Horned viper

Home: hot, dry deserts
Food: mice and lizards
Colour: sand-coloured
Is it poisonous? Yes
Special body parts: two large, pointed scales above its eyes that look like little horns.
Amazing fact: a horned viper moves by flipping itself across the sand.

Puzzles

Here are some puzzles to try. Look back in the book to help you find the answers.

Close-up!

We've zoomed in on some of the snakes that you met earlier. Can you tell which ones they are?

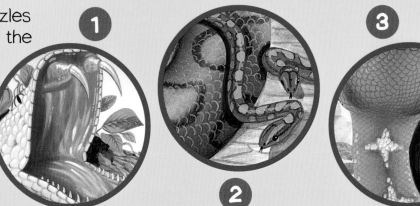

Hide and seek

There are four pythons in this picture. Where are they hiding?

Spot the difference

Look carefully at these baby snakes hatching out of their eggs. Can you spot four differences between the pictures?

a

b

In a tangle

How many different snakes are there in this tangle? Here's a clue – look at the patterned scales.

Index

Created and published by
Two-Can Publishing Ltd
346 Old Street
London
EC1V 9RB

Consultant: Mark Caddy
Main illustrations: Mike Atkinson
Cartoon illustrations: Alan Rowe
Photographs: front cover Papilio Photographic;
p5 Planet Earth Pictures; p9 Natural History
Photographic Agency; p13 Tony Stone Images.

ISBN 1-85434-789-6

Dewey Decimal Classification 597.96

Paperback 10 9 8 7 6 5 4 3 2 1

A catalogue record for this book is available from the
British Library.

Printed in Hong Kong by Wing King Tong